DINOSAUR FACT DIG

TYRANNOSAURUS REX AND ITS RELATIVES
THE NEED-TO-KNOW FACTS

BY
MEGAN COOLEY PETERSON

Consultant: Mathew J. Wedel, PhD
Associate Professor
Western University of Health Services

CAPSTONE PRESS
a capstone imprint

A+ Books are published by Capstone Press,
1710 Roe Crest Drive, North Mankato, Minnesota 56003
www.mycapstone.com

Library of Congress Cataloging-in-Publication Data
Peterson, Megan Cooley, author.
Tyrannosaurus rex and its relatives : the need-to-know facts / by Megan Cooley Peterson.
pages cm. – (A+ books. Dinosaur fact dig)
Audience: Ages 4–8.
Audience: K to grade 3.
Summary: "Full-color images and simple text introduce young readers to different dinosaurs
related to Tyrannosaurus rex, including their physical characteristics, habitats, and diets"–
Provided by publisher.
Includes bibliographical references and index.
ISBN 978-1-4914-9650-3 (library binding)
ISBN 978-1-4914-9657-2 (paperback)
ISBN 978-1-4914-9663-3 (eBook PDF)
1. Tyrannosaurus rex–Juvenile literature. 2. Dinosaurs–Juvenile literature. I. Title.
QE862.S3.P485 2016
567.91–dc23   2015028921

EDITORIAL CREDITS:
Michelle Hasselius, editor; Kazuko Collins, designer;
Wanda Winch, media researcher; Gene Bentdahl, production specialist

IMAGE CREDITS: All images by Jon Hughes except: MapArt (maps), Shutterstock: Elena
Elisseeva, green gingko leaf, Jiang Hongyan, yellow gingko leaf, Taigi, paper background

Printed in US.
007535CGS16

**NOTE TO PARENTS, TEACHERS,
AND LIBRARIANS:**
This Dinosaur Fact Dig book uses full-color
images and a nonfiction format to introduce
the concept of Tyrannosaurus rex relatives.
Tyrannosaurus Rex and Its Relatives is designed
to be read aloud to a pre-reader or to be read
independently by an early reader. Images help
listeners and early readers understand the text
and concepts discussed. The book encourages
further learning by including the following
sections: Table of Contents, Glossary, Read
More, Internet Sites, Critical Thinking Using the
Common Core, and Index. Early readers may
need assistance using these features.

TABLE OF CONTENTS

Roar! Tyrannosaurus rex was one of the fiercest dinosaurs that ever lived. This deadly hunter had sharp teeth and strong jaws. But did you know that a birdlike dinosaur with no teeth was related to T. rex?

Tyrannosaurus rex and its relatives lived between 160 million and 65 million years ago. This group includes the toothless Gallimimus and the powerful Daspletosaurus. Some T. Rex relatives hunted dinosaurs. Others ate insects and fruit. Each was amazing in its own way.

ALBERTOSAURUS

PRONOUNCED: al-BURR-toe-SAWR-us

NAME MEANING: Alberta reptile; fossils were discovered in Alberta, Canada

TIME PERIOD LIVED: Late Cretaceous Period, about 70 million years ago

LENGTH: 28.2 feet (8.6 meters)

WEIGHT: 2.8 tons (2.5 metric tons)

TYPE OF EATER: carnivore

PHYSICAL FEATURES: sharp teeth, two fingers on each small arm

Geologist Joseph Burr Tyrrell discovered the first **ALBERTOSAURUS** fossil in 1884. It was Canada's first known meat-eating dinosaur.

ALBERTOSAURUS probably hunted in packs to attack large herbivores. Young Albertosaurus may have chased prey toward stronger adults.

Albertosaurus lived in what are now Montana and Alberta, Canada.

ALBERTOSAURUS had 60 curved, serrated teeth. It mainly hunted herbivores, but it was also a scavenger.

N
W   E
S

where this dinosaur lived

ALIORAMUS

PRONOUNCED: AL-ee-OH-rah-MUS

NAME MEANING: other branch

TIME PERIOD LIVED: Late Cretaceous Period, about 70 million years ago

LENGTH: 19 feet (5.8 m)

WEIGHT: 1500 pounds (680 kilograms)

TYPE OF EATER: carnivore

PHYSICAL FEATURES: long jaws, bumpy horns on nose, ran on two legs

ALIORAMUS was one of the biggest hunters of its time. But it was only about half the size of Tyrannosaurus rex.

Alioramus lived in the forests of what is now Mongolia.

N
W — E
S

where this dinosaur lived

ALIORAMUS had eyes that faced forward, like today's owls and other birds of prey.

ALIORAMUS had more than 75 teeth, the most of any tyrannosaur.

ALVAREZSAURUS

PRONOUNCED: AL-vuh-rez-SAWR-us

NAME MEANING: Alvarez's reptile, in honor of historian Don Gregorio Alvarez

TIME PERIOD LIVED: Late Cretaceous Period, about 85 million years ago

LENGTH: 3.3 feet (1 m)

WEIGHT: 6.5 pounds (3 kg)

TYPE OF EATER: carnivore

PHYSICAL FEATURES: long legs and tail, one strong claw on each hand

Similar to today's anteaters, **ALVAREZSAURUS** dug into ant nests with its strong claws. It may have also had a long tongue that it used to pull ants and termites from their nests.

Alvarezsaurus lived in what is now Argentina.

N
W   E
S

☐ **where this dinosaur lived**

ALVAREZSAURUS was about the size of a turkey.

ALVAREZSAURUS belonged to a group of dinosaurs called Alvarezsaurs. Dinosaurs in this group had a single claw on each strong arm.

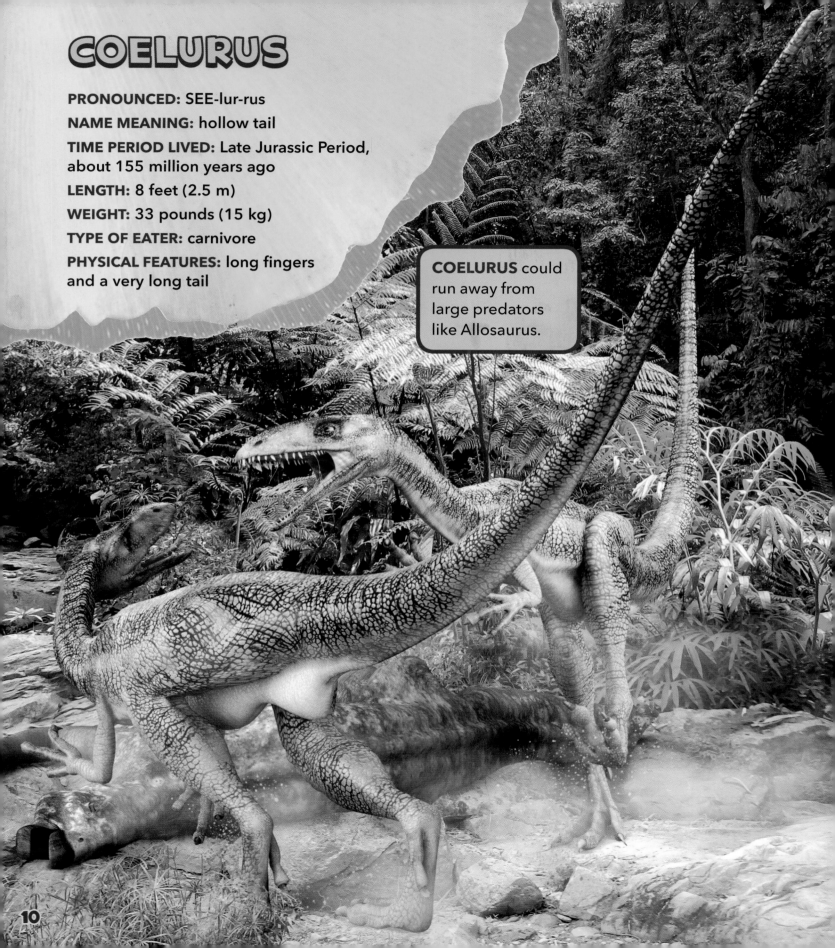

COELURUS

PRONOUNCED: SEE-lur-rus

NAME MEANING: hollow tail

TIME PERIOD LIVED: Late Jurassic Period, about 155 million years ago

LENGTH: 8 feet (2.5 m)

WEIGHT: 33 pounds (15 kg)

TYPE OF EATER: carnivore

PHYSICAL FEATURES: long fingers and a very long tail

COELURUS could run away from large predators like Allosaurus.

COELURUS belonged to a group of dinosaurs called coelurosaurs. Dinosaurs in this group had larger brains than other dinosaurs their size.

Coelurus lived in what are now Wyoming and Utah.

N
W E
S

☐ where this dinosaur lived

COELURUS hunted small animals and dinosaurs.

COMPSOGNATHUS

PRONOUNCED: COMP-sog-NAY-thus

NAME MEANING: delicate jaw

TIME PERIOD LIVED: Late Jurassic Period, about 150 million years ago

LENGTH: 4 feet (1.2 m)

WEIGHT: 5.5 pounds (2.5 kg)

TYPE OF EATER: carnivore

PHYSICAL FEATURES: long legs and tail, lightweight body, short teeth

A **COMPSOGNATHUS** fossil was found with the skeleton of the fast-running lizard Bavarisaurus in its stomach.

COMPSOGNATHUS was about the size of a chicken.

COMPSOGNATHUS hunted small lizards and bugs.

Compsognathus lived in forests and on beaches in France and Germany.

N
W   E
S

where this dinosaur lived

DASPLETOSAURUS

PRONOUNCED: das-PLEET-o-SAWR-us

NAME MEANING: frightful reptile

TIME PERIOD LIVED: Late Cretaceous Period, about 80 million years ago

LENGTH: 30 feet (9 m)

WEIGHT: 2.8 tons (2.5 metric tons)

TYPE OF EATER: carnivore

PHYSICAL FEATURES: big, sharp teeth and a strong body

Daspletosaurus lived in what are now Montana, New Mexico, and Alberta, Canada.

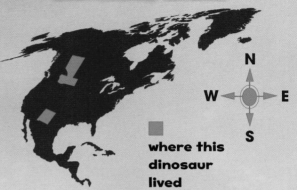

where this dinosaur lived

N
W   E
S

DASPLETOSAURUS is more closely related to Tyrannosaurus rex than any other dinosaur.

Many **DASPLETOSAURUS** fossils were found with healed injuries. The injuries show the dinosaurs bit each other's noses.

Similar to today's lions, **DASPLETOSAURUS** lived and hunted in family packs. The packs killed large herbivores, such as Triceratops.

EOTYRANNUS

PRONOUNCED: EE-o-tye-RAN-us

NAME MEANING: dawn tyrant

TIME PERIOD LIVED: Early Cretaceous Period, about 130 million years ago

LENGTH: 14.8 feet (4.5 m)

WEIGHT: 441 pounds (200 kg)

TYPE OF EATER: carnivore

PHYSICAL FEATURES: long legs and arms, had feathers but couldn't fly

EOTYRANNUS was one of the smallest meat-eating dinosaurs in Europe.

EOTYRANNUS hunted small dinosaurs and animals. It made quick, deep bites into its prey.

Eotyrannus lived in what is now England.

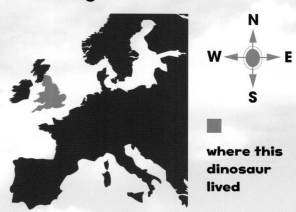

N
W E
S

■ where this dinosaur lived

Close relatives of **EOTYRANNUS** were discovered in China. These dinosaurs had feathers.

EOTYRANNUS was named in 2001.

EOTYRANNUS could run fast. It used its speed to run away from bigger predators, such as Baryonx and Neovenator.

GALLIMIMUS

PRONOUNCED: GAL-i-MY-mus

NAME MEANING: chicken mimic

TIME PERIOD LIVED: Late Cretaceous Period, about 70 million years ago

LENGTH: 20 feet (6 m)

WEIGHT: 1000 pounds (450 kg)

TYPE OF EATER: omnivore

PHYSICAL FEATURES: long legs, beaklike snout with no teeth

GALLIMIMUS was hunted by predators such as Tarbosaurus bataar.

Similar to ostriches today, **GALLIMIMUS** could run very fast.

Gallimimus lived in the plains and forests of what is now Mongolia.

N
W — E
S

where this dinosaur lived

GALLIMIMUS had comblike edges on its snout. The dinosaur may have used its snout to filter out food from rivers and lakes. It ate small animals, fruit, and leaves.

GALLIMIMUS had three clawed fingers on each hand. Feathers covered the dinosaur's body.

GUANLONG

PRONOUNCED: gwahn-LAWNG

NAME MEANING: crowned dragon

TIME PERIOD LIVED: Late Jurassic Period, about 160 million years ago

LENGTH: 9.8 feet (3 m)

WEIGHT: 250 pounds (113 kg)

TYPE OF EATER: carnivore

PHYSICAL FEATURES: colorful crest on its head, strong hands with a sharp claw on each finger

GUANLONG was a small dinosaur. It was about the size of a dog.

GUANLONG has the most complete skeleton of any early tyrannosauroid so far.

GUANLONG used its colorful crest to attract other dinosaurs.

Guanlong lived in what is now China.

N
W
E
S

where this dinosaur lived

LABOCANIA

PRONOUNCED: LAB-o-KAN-ee-uh

NAME MEANING: La Bocana Roja lizard, because fossils were discovered at the La Bocana Roja Formation

TIME PERIOD LIVED: Late Cretaceous Period, about 75 million years ago

LENGTH: 23 feet (7 m)

WEIGHT: 1.7 tons (1.5 metric tons)

TYPE OF EATER: carnivore

PHYSICAL FEATURES: thick snout and jaw, walked on two legs

Labocania lived in the forests of what is now Mexico.

N
W E
S

□ where this dinosaur lived

Only a few **LABOCANIA** fossils have been discovered, including a partial skull.

LABOCANIA had huge jaws and sharp teeth. One bite was often deadly.

LABOCANIA was the first theropod discovered in Mexico. Theropods were meat-eating dinosaurs that included tyrannosaurs, raptors, and birds.

ORNITHOMIMUS

PRONOUNCED: OR-ni-thuh-MY-mus

NAME MEANING: bird mimic

TIME PERIOD LIVED: Late Cretaceous Period, about 65 million years ago

LENGTH: 11.5 feet (3.5 m)

WEIGHT: 350 pounds (160 kg)

TYPE OF EATER: omnivore

PHYSICAL FEATURES: tiny head, long legs and neck, beak with no teeth

The dinosaur's body was covered with feathers. It looked like today's ostrich.

ORNITHOMIMUS had a beak covered with keratin. It ate fruit and insects.

Ornithomimus lived in what are now Colorado, Wyoming, South Dakota, and Utah. This dinosaur also lived in Alberta and Saskatchewan, Canada.

In 1892 O.C. Marsh thought he had discovered a giant new species of ORNITHOMIMUS. He actually found the hip and leg bones of a Tyrannosaurus rex. These two dinosaurs had similar back leg bones.

where this
dinosaur
lived

N
W E
S

25

TIMIMUS

PRONOUNCED: tee-MYE-mus

NAME MEANING: Tim's mimic, named after the son of the scientist who discovered it

TIME PERIOD LIVED: Early Cretaceous Period, about 100 million years ago

LENGTH: 9.8 feet (3 m)

WEIGHT: 120 pounds (54 kg)

TYPE OF EATER: carnivore

PHYSICAL FEATURES: strong back legs, sharp claws

TIMIMUS fossils were discovered in Dinosaur Cove in southern Australia.

Scientists are not sure how to classify **TIMIMUS**. Some think it belonged to a group of dinosaurs called coelurosaurs. Dinosaurs in this group were hunters with narrow hands and large brains. Others think the dinosaur was an ornithomimosaur. These dinosaurs had small beaks and did not hunt.

TIMIMUS may have hibernated during the winter. Australia was closer to the South Pole during the Cretaceous Period.

Timimus lived in what is now Australia.

N

W E

S

where this dinosaur lived

TYRANNOSAURUS REX

PRONOUNCED: tie-RAN-uh-SAWR-us REX

NAME MEANING: king tyrant reptile

TIME PERIOD LIVED: Late Cretaceous Period, about 70 million years ago

LENGTH: 40 feet (12 m)

WEIGHT: 9 tons (8.2 metric tons)

TYPE OF EATER: carnivore

PHYSICAL FEATURES: big head with sharp teeth, tiny arms, sharp claws, and a long tail

TYRANNOSAURUS REX had excellent vision.

TYRANNOSAURUS REX was a predator that spent most of its time hunting. This dinosaur was also a scavenger.

TYRANNOSAURUS REX was the largest dinosaur in this group.

Tyrannosaurus rex lived in western North America.

N
W   E
S

where this dinosaur lived

GLOSSARY

BEAK (BEEK)—the hard, pointed part of an animal's mouth

CARNIVORE (KAR-nuh-vor)—an animal that eats only meat

CREST (KREST)—a flat plate of bone

CRETACEOUS PERIOD (krah-TAY-shus PIHR-ee-uhd)—the third period of the Mesozoic Era; the Cretaceous Period was from 145 to 65 million years ago

FOSSIL (FOSS-uhl)—the remains of an animal or plant from millions of years ago that have turned to rock

HERBIVORE (HUR-buh-vor)—an animal that eats only plants

HIBERNATE (HYE-bur-nate)—to spend winter in a deep sleep; animals hibernate to survive low temperatures and lack of food

JURASSIC PERIOD (ju-RASS-ik PIHR-ee-uhd)—the second period of the Mesozoic Era; the Jurassic Period was from 200 to 145 million years ago

KERATIN (KAIR-uh-tin)—the hard substance that makes up a person's fingernails and toenails

OMNIVORE (OM-nuh-vor)—an animal that eats both plants and animals

PACK (PAK)—a small group of animals that hunts together

PREDATOR (PRED-uh-tur)—an animal that hunts another animal for food

PREY (PRAY)—an animal hunted by another animal for food

PRONOUNCE (proh-NOUNSS)—to say a word in a certain way

SCAVENGER (SKAV-uhn-jer)—an animal that eats animals that are already dead

SERRATED (SER-ay-tid)—saw-toothed

SNOUT (SNOUT)—the long front part of an animal's head; the snout includes the nose, mouth, and jaws

CRITICAL THINKING USING THE COMMON CORE

1. How did Eotyrannus stay safe around large predators such as Baryonx and Neovenator? (Key Ideas and Details)

2. Scientists are not sure how to classify Timimus. What two dinosaur groups could this dinosaur belong to? (Key Ideas and Details)

3. Only a few Labocania fossils have been discovered. What is a fossil? (Craft and Structure)

READ MORE

Carr, Aaron. *T-rex.* Discovering Dinosaurs. New York: AV2 by Weigl, 2013.

Pallotta, Jerry. *Tyrannosaurus Rex vs. Velociraptor.* New York: Scholastic, 2010.

Wegwerth, A.L. *Tyrannosaurus Rex.* Little Paleontologist. North Mankato, Minn.: Capstone Press, 2015.

INTERNET SITES

FactHound offers a safe, fun way to find Internet sites related to this book. All of the sites on FactHound have been researched by our staff.

Here's all you do:

Visit *www.facthound.com*

Type in this code: 9781491496503

Check out projects, games and lots more at
www.capstonekids.com

INDEX